TREASURY OF LITERATURE

PRACTICE BOOK

SEA OF WONDER

HARCOURT BRACE & COMPANY

Orlando   Atlanta   Austin   Boston   San Francisco   Chicago   Dallas   New York
Toronto   London

CONTENTS

Printed in the United States of America

ISBN 0-15-301294-3

4 5 6 7 8 9 10   030   97   96   95

Name _____

Read the letter. Use clues in it to decide the meaning of
each underlined word. Write each word beside its meaning.

Dear Mom,

    Last night, Aunt Mary and I went looking for raccoons.
We walked to the <u>clearing</u> called Open Meadow. Then we
watched from the nearby trees. The moonlight shining on a
pine made a big <u>shadow</u> across the grass. We stood so still,
we must have looked like stone <u>statues</u>. Aunt Mary said to be
<u>quiet</u> so the raccoons wouldn't hear us. Suddenly, an animal
ran by. It was <u>furry</u>, but its hair wasn't long or grayish brown,
so I knew it couldn't be a raccoon. Aunt Mary whispered,
"What was it?" I didn't know, so I just <u>shrugged</u> my shoulders.

    Aunt Mary was afraid I'd be disappointed when I didn't see
a raccoon. We had fun, though. And guess what? Tonight we
are going <u>owling</u>! I hope I see a screech owl.

          Love,

1. covered with hair _____

2. area free of trees but surrounded by them _____

3. shade made by something coming between light and a surface _____

4. raised one's shoulders _____

5. looking for owls _____

6. carvings of rock _____

7. making very little noise _____

Name_____

Write a summary of the story "Owl Moon." Fill in the blanks below. Add your own pictures.

Who the characters are: _____

_____

What they want: _____

What they do: _____

_____

_____

What happens at the end:

_____

_____

_____

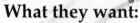

Write one sentence telling about the feelings in this story.

_____

_____

Name _____

A. **Find each simile from the story and draw a line under it. The first one has been done for you.**

  1. The owl glided <u>like a dark kite</u> in the night.

  2. A train whistle blew, long and low, like a sad, sad song.

  3. When their voices faded away, it was as quiet as a dream.

  4. The owl lifted off the branch like a shadow without sound.

  5. I could feel the cold, as if someone's icy hand was palm-down on my back.

B. **Complete these similes.**

  1. The snow crunched under our boots with a sound like _____

_____.

  2. Waiting for the owl, I was as nervous as _____

_____.

  3. The owl's hoot sounded like _____

_____.

  4. The barn owl swiveled its head like _____

_____.

  5. A cloud drifted across the moon like _____

_____.

  6. The night was as dark as _____

_____.

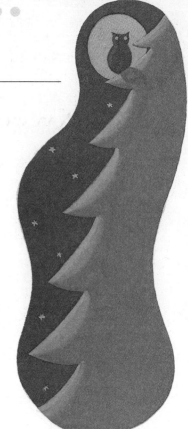

Name _____

A. **Read the following paragraph. Circle the articles.**

Last week my mother and I saw an owl in the
trees behind our house. It was evening and the air
was just beginning to turn cool. We were walking
down the gravel path from the shed to our house.
Suddenly, we heard a strange sound. My mother
froze, her eyes on an old pine tree. I followed her
eyes and caught a glimpse of the owl as it took off.

B. **Complete each sentence by circling the correct article in parentheses ( ).**

1. My teacher assigned (a/an) report about wild animals.

2. I'm going to write about (the/an) bald eagle.

3. I once saw (a/an) eagle when I was camping with my family.

4. My mother says that bald eagles are (the/an) endangered species.

5. My father gave me (an/a) pair of binoculars for birdwatching.

6. (The/An) cat next door also likes to watch birds.

••

SUMMARIZING
the **L**EARNING   The adjectives *a, an,* and *the* are called _____.

Use *a* before a word that begins with a _____ sound. Use *an*

before a word that begins with a _____ sound.

Name_____

Read about making a bird feeder. Draw a line under all the words that are clues about when to do each step. Then answer the questions.

You can make a treat for the birds in your neighborhood. Before you begin, you will need to get bird seed, peanut butter, a big pine cone, and string. First, dump the seeds and the peanut butter into a bowl and mix them together. Then, spread the gooey bird food on the pine cone. Next, tie string on the top of the pine cone. Finally, hang the feeder on a tree branch. After you hang the cone up, all you have to do is watch! The birds will love their yummy treat.

1. When should you get the bird seed? _____

2. When should you spread the bird food on the pine cone?

before _____

after _____

3. Think about what you already know. Why do you think you should add the string after you spread the peanut butter mix?

_____

_____

4. What is the last thing to do to enjoy your bird feeder? _____

SUMMARIZING the **L**EARNING   When I read, I try to understand the order in which things happen. I watch for word clues like _____

_____.

Name _____

Look carefully at the book pages and answer the questions.

Title page

Copyright ©1991 by
Wildlife Publishers
All rights reserved.
ISBN 193759365

Copyright page

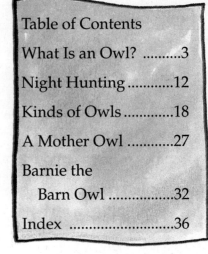

Table of Contents
What Is an Owl? 3
Night Hunting 12
Kinds of Owls 18
A Mother Owl 27
Barnie the
   Barn Owl 32
Index 36

Table of Contents

1. On what page can you find the name of a book? _____

2. What is this book called? _____

3. Who is the author? _____

4. Where can you find publishing information? _____

5. In what year was this book published? _____

6. Who published it? _____

7. Where can you find a summary of what is in a book?

   _____

8. Name two subjects that are covered in this book.

   _____

9. Where would you look to find out what page has information

   about owl feathers? _____

Look at the index for *Our Owls*. Answer the questions.

INDEX

Baby owls, 28
    See also *chicks*
Burrowing owls, 19
Camouflage, 8
Chicks
    Flying lessons for, 29
    Food for, 31
    Protection of, 31
Eyes
    Position of, 5
    Sight in, 4
Food
    Birds and fish, 14
    Mice, 12

Great gray owl, 23
Hearing, 11, 15
Nesting
    Areas for, 29
    Materials used, 30
Snowy owls, 25
Territory, 6
Ural owls, 26
Wings
    Feathers in, 7
    Span, 5
Winter habitat, 8

---

1. In what order is information listed? _____

2. On what page will you find information on snowy owls? _____

3. You want information on baby owls. What other word should you look

under? _____

4. On what page would you find out how chicks are protected? _____

5. Name three pages that talk about owl food. _____

6. On what page will you find out what owls use to build nests? _____

Name_____

Read the words and their meanings. Then imagine that you are a raccoon. Answer the questions using the word or words in parentheses ( ) in sentences of your own.

attracted drawn to, interested in	**shallow** not deep
bandit robber	**chuckle** to make a soft, laughing sound
created made	**marshes** low, wet land
recognize to know or identify	

Excuse me, sir. What sound do raccoons make?

(chuckle)

How can I be sure that you are a raccoon?

(recognize, bandit)

Mr. Raccoon, this dam wasn't always here at the pond. Do you know where it came from?

(created)

Where are we most likely to see a raccoon?

(marshes, shallow)

Can you tell us why you came to the pond tonight?

(attracted)

Name _____

Fill in the first two columns of the **KWL** chart before you read. Add to the second column during reading. Complete the chart after you have read the story.

K	W	L
What I Know	**What I Want to Know**	**What I Learned**

What was the most important idea in this story? _____

_____

Name_____

A. Read the paragraph. Draw a line under all the sound words.

    Drip, drip, drip. Rain was pouring down through the trees. My shoes squished with each step. I blew my nose into my hankie with a big honk. I was cold, but I just had to find my pet crow. She had fluttered past me out the door more than an hour ago. The only sounds were the rustling leaves and the plop-plop of raindrops. I whistled. "Jeanette!" I screeched. "Where are you?" Finally I heard, "Caw! Caw!" and my bird landed, smack on my head.

B. Rewrite these sentences. Change the underlined words. Use a sound word in your new sentences.

1. When I heard the grunt, I knew there was a pig in there.

    _____

2. The tree fell with a crash.

    _____

3. The goose gave a loud honk as it flew.

    _____

4. The raccoon chittered as it looked down at me.

    _____

5. "I think I've made a mistake!" the tracker whispered.

    _____

Name _____

A. **Read the following paragraph. Underline the adjectives that make comparisons.**

I think a walk outside is more interesting than an hour of TV. I enjoy trying to spot different birds in the forest. Some birds are rarer than others. For example, owls are the most difficult birds to find. Blue jays are bolder than many birds, so they are easier to spot.

B. **Circle the correct form of the word in parentheses ( ).**

1. I think dogs are (friendlier/friendliest) than cats.

2. My dog looks (happiest/happier) than my cat when I get home.

3. Dogs are (most/more) obedient than cats.

4. On the other hand, cats are (easier/easiest) to hold in your lap than dogs are.

5. My sister thinks that birds make the (more/most) interesting pets.

6. I don't like birds because they are the (noisiest/noisier) kind of pet to have.

••

SUMMARIZING
the **L**EARNING   Adjectives can describe by _____ people, animals, places, or things. Add _____ to adjectives to compare two things, or use the word _____. Add _____ to adjectives to compare more than two things, or use the word _____.

Name_____

Study the diagram and then answer the questions.

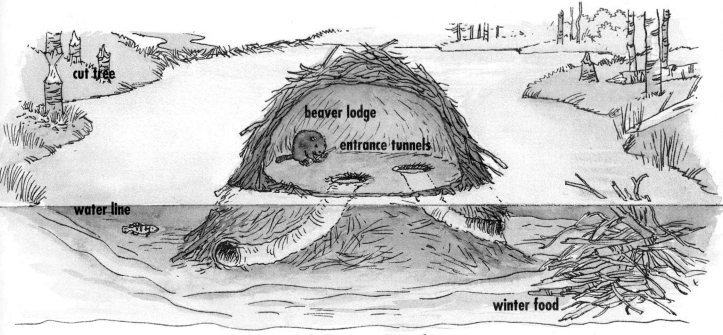

cut tree

beaver lodge

entrance tunnels

water line

winter food

A Beaver Pond

1. What is this a picture of? _____

2. What is a beaver home called? _____

3. How many entrances does a beaver home have? _____

4. Where do beavers keep their winter food?_____

_____

5. Is a beaver's living area above or below the waterline? _____

6. A beaver's winter food is called a *cache*. Label the cache on the diagram.

7. Add a beaver to the diagram. Label what it is doing. _____

_____

GO ON

Name _____

Study the chart and the table. Answer the questions.

Two Rodents

	Animal family	Fur	Size	Where they live	Food
Muskrats	rodents	light brown	16-26 inches	streams, ponds, and rivers	cattails, roots
Beavers	rodents	dark to golden brown	36-48 inches	rivers and streams near woodlands	bark, twigs, leaves, roots

Beaver Sightings on Cooper's Pond						
	Jan.	Feb.	Mar.	Apr.	May	June
1990	4	4	3	6	8	10
1991	4	5	4	7	9	11

1. The purpose of the information in the chart is to show _____

_____ .

2. How many beavers were seen on the pond in February of 1990? _____

3. Is the population of beavers at the pond becoming larger or smaller?

_____ How do you know? _____

4. You see an animal at the pond. It is brown and about 24 inches long.

It's eating roots. What is it? _____

How do you know? _____

Name_____

A. Look at this set of encyclopedias. Write the number of the volume where you would find information on each topic.

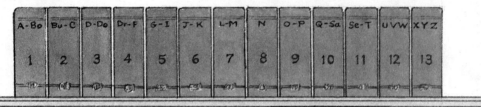

1. beavers _____

2. what turtles eat _____

3. ducks _____

4. what otter tracks look like _____

5. uses, if any, for cattails _____

6. stages in the life of a dragonfly _____

7. different kinds of plants that grow in ponds _____

B. Look at the guide words on these encyclopedia pages. Write one entry word that might be found between each pair of guide words.

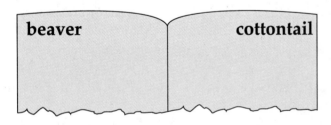

GO ON

Name _____

Study the encyclopedia index and answer the questions.

Animal	**Anise** [plant] **A:423**
Animal A:400 *with pictures and maps*	**Anise swallowtail** [insect]
Extinct animals **E:465**	See *butterfly* **B:622**
Fur **F:561**	**Ankylosaur**
Migration **M:138**	See *dinosaur* **D:155**
Tracks	**Anna, Antonio Lopez A:509**
Bear picture on **T:193**	**Antarctica** *with pictures* **A:538**
Deer picture on **T:193**	**Anteater A:545**
Mouse picture on **T:193**	**Antenna** See *insects* **I:401**
Rabbit picture on **T:193**	**Anthracite A:630**
Animal training A:405	Also see *coal* **C:694**
Dog training **D:776**	**Antler**
Animated cartoon	See *deer* **D:482**
See *cartoon* **C:221**	See *reindeer picture on* **R:15**
See *Disney, Walt* **D:323**	

1. Where would you find information on anteaters?

volume _____, page _____

2. Where might you find information on training a cat?

volume _____, page _____   A dog? volume _____, page _____

3. Under what entry words would you find information

on animated cartoons? _____

4. What animal tracks does this encyclopedia have

pictures of? _____

5. In what two places can you find information about animated cartoons?

volume _____, page _____   volume _____, page _____

6. What volume tells about anise? _____ What is it? _____

Name _____

A. Read the words in the box and think about their
meanings. Write each word next to the riddle it answers.

bolts	**idea**	**nuts**	**sprinkling**
bored	**nervous**	**reminded**	**wriggled**

1. Think, think, think hard, please.
   A light bulb comes on in your head with one of these. _____

2. Each of us is shaped like a fat pin.
   Sometimes a screwdriver can screw us in. _____

3. If you ever feel like me,
   You're as jumpy and fearful as you can be. _____

4. Water is doing this when it's scattering.
   Rain is doing this when it's spattering. _____

5. You asked me to recall
   When I didn't remember at all. _____

6. Here's a HO-HUM feeling for you,
   When it seems as if there's nothing to do. _____

7. We hold bolts tight with all our might. _____

8. I twisted and twitched and squirmed. Just look.

   I moved like a wiggly worm on a hook. _____

B. For each numbered item, write one sentence using
the set of words in parentheses ( ).

1. (nuts, bolts) _____

2. (bored, idea) _____

Name _____

Think about what happened in the story "A Day When Frogs Wear Shoes," and then fill in the cause-effect chain below.

Julian, Huey, and Gloria are bored.

They decide to visit Julian's dad at his repair shop.

Julian says they are hiking, but then Huey says that

Julian, Huey, and Gloria help Julian's dad so

Julian's dad says the frogs are down the bank a ways, so

Julian's dad tells the children to put on their shoes. When they do,

Name _____

A. Underline the predicate and circle the action verb in each sentence. The first sentence is done for you.

The river (flows) gently for several miles. It carries leaves and small branches. Shallow water moves more quickly. Frogs swim in pools on the sides of the river. A raccoon drinks from the river.

B. Write a sentence to describe what is happening in each picture. Use one action verb in each sentence.

_____

_____

_____

_____

_____

_____

SUMMARIZING the LEARNING   A verb is the main word in the _____ of a sentence. A verb that tells what the subject does is an _____ .

Name _____

A. Read each sentence. On each line, write *F* for *fact* or
O for *opinion.*

_____ Many people spend time in the summer watching baseball.

_____ There have been baseball teams in the United States for
more than 100 years.

_____ Watching baseball is the best way to spend a day.

_____ The game is so exciting!

_____ Some pitchers can throw a ball at a speed greater than
90 miles per hour.

_____ Most baseball games last about three or four hours.

_____ Americans will always play baseball!

B. Write one fact and one opinion about these things
people do. Then complete the page.

hiking

Fact _____

Opinion _____

drinking lemonade

Fact _____

Opinion _____

SUMMARIZING
the **L**EARNING   Something that really happened or can be proved is

a(n) _____.

Something that is a belief, a judgment, or a feeling is a(n) _____.

Name_____

Study the picture of the encyclopedia and answer the questions.

A	B	C-D	E-Fo	Fr-H	I-K	La-Ma	Me-Mu	N-O	P-Q	R-Sn	So-T	U-W	XYZ	Index
1	2	3	4	5	6	7	8	9	10	11	12	13	14	15

1. How many volumes are there in this encyclopedia? _____

2. What volume would you use to learn about frogs? _____

3. The entry for frogs says "see also AMPHIBIANS." Where

    would you look for that entry? _____

4. What volume would you use to look up sandals? _____

5. If there is no entry for sandals, what volume would you look in

    next for information about them? _____

6. Why would you look there? _____

    _____

7. There is a short entry for tracks in this encyclopedia. Write two

    guide words that might appear on that page. _____

    _____

Name_____

Read the paragraph below. Use clues in the sentences to figure out what the underlined words mean. Write the meanings.

The day was a real scorcher —100 degrees in the shade! I had wet drops of perspiration on my forehead. I love cool weather, but I dislike the heat. Jill wanted to do a rain dance, but it was too hot for exercise. A workout like that is for chilly weather. Andy wanted to walk to the beach. But I couldn't stand to tramp there in the heat. I think my idea was the best notion we had. I wanted to spend the day at the supermarket. Why go to a food store, you ask? The coolers! Their frigid air would cool us off in no time flat!

1. A scorcher is _____.

2. Perspiration is _____ .

3. Exercise is _____ .

4. To tramp means _____.

5. A notion is _____.

6. A supermarket is _____ .

7. Frigid means _____.

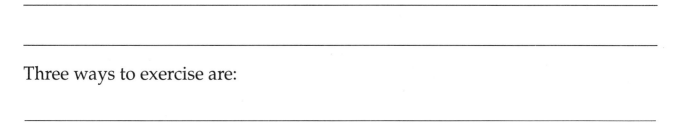

Two notions I have are:

_____

_____

Three ways to exercise are:

_____

Name _____

Armadillo is telling his friends about his travels. Fill in the words to complete his sentences. The words you need are in the box.

beyond	continent	landscape	entire	homeward

I flew across the whole

_____ of North America!

From up high I could see

_____ mountain ranges.

When I looked _____
the mountains, I saw green valleys.

Now I want to travel _____ .

My favorite _____ of all
is the one near my own home!

With your classmates, create a mural that shows where Armadillo went on his trip. Include captions that explain the different sections of the mural. Use all the vocabulary words in your captions.

Name _____

Think about "The Armadillo from Amarillo."
**Tell what happened by filling in the
story frame.**

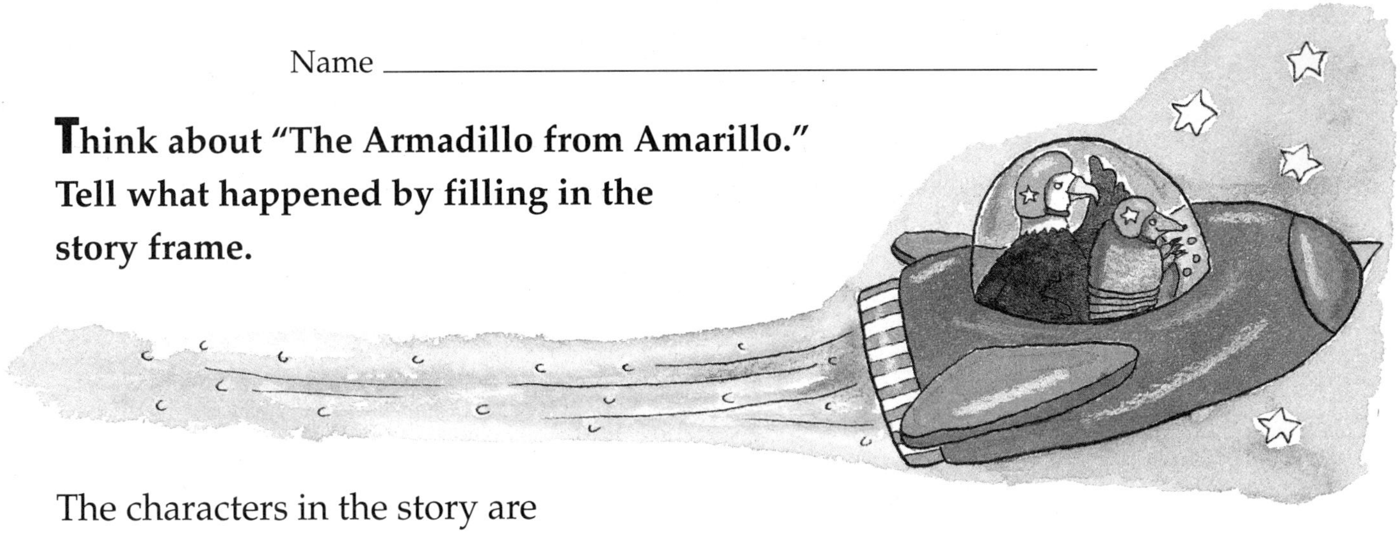

The characters in the story are

_____.

What the characters want to do is

_____

_____.

What they do is

_____

_____

_____.

At the end,

_____.

What I learned by reading this story is

_____

_____.

Name _____

Armadillo is teaching Junior what he learned on his
trip. Use the words below to help him.

canyon
state
continent
woodland
planet
plains

1. A word meaning the same thing as "flatlands" is _____.

2. A place that has many trees is called a _____.

3. A _____ is a part of a country, and it rhymes with "plate."

4. Africa, which has many countries, is a _____.

5. The earth is a _____.

6. A narrow valley is a _____.

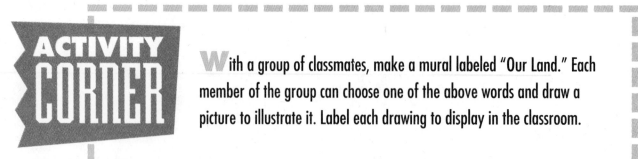

ACTIVITY CORNER

With a group of classmates, make a mural labeled "Our Land." Each member of the group can choose one of the above words and draw a picture to illustrate it. Label each drawing to display in the classroom.

Name _____

A. Circle the main verb and underline the helping verb in each sentence. The first sentence is done for you.

Tortoise has (traveled) to Mexico. I have visited that country, too. Tortoise and I have read many books about Mexican history together. I had planned a trip there with Tortoise. But my boss has given me too much work, and I have stayed home. Tortoise has written me a postcard.

B. Circle the correct helping verb in parentheses ( ).

1. Teo (has/have) lived in Amarillo for ten years.

2. He (have/has) built a house at the edge of the city.

3. Teo's parents also (has/have) built a nice home in Amarillo.

Write a sentence about a place you have visited or read about. Use a helping verb in your sentence.

_____

_____

● ●

SUMMARIZING
the **L**EARNING   The most important verb in a sentence is the

_____. A verb that helps the main verb show action in a sentence

is called a _____ .

Name _____

Study the map and the table. Then answer the questions
on the next page.

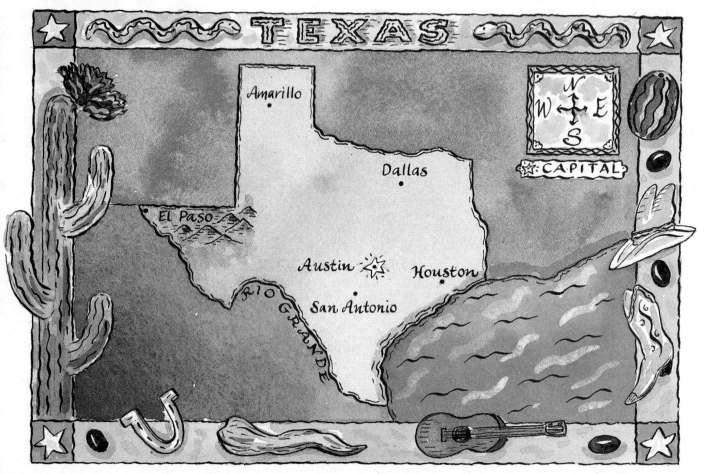

MILES TRAVELED				
	Week 1	**Week 2**	**Week 3**	**Week 4**
Mornings	7	4	8	5
Afternoons	5	6	6	8
Total	12	10	14	13

Name _____

1. Armadillo visited the capital city of Texas. What is its name?

_____

2. What Texas city is the farthest west?

_____

3. If Armadillo had gone south from Amarillo, what river would he have crossed?

_____

4. Are there mountains north or south of Amarillo?

_____

5. How far did Armadillo travel during the afternoons of Week 2?

_____

6. In which week did he travel the farthest?

_____

7. How many miles did Armadillo travel in Week 4?

_____

8. In which week did Armadillo travel the least?

_____

With a group of classmates, find out more about the Texas cities on the map. Each person can then present facts about one city.

Name _____

A. Think about the story "The Armadillo from Amarillo." Write *before* or *after* to complete the sentences.

1. Armadillo packed up his things _____ he left home.

2. He went to the top of a tall tower _____ he reached the city of San Antonio.

3. He held on to Eagle's neck _____ he hopped onto her back.

4. Eagle and Armadillo flew high enough to see New Mexico _____ they could see all of the earth.

B. Complete the sentences to tell what happened in the story.

1. Before Armadillo met Eagle, he _____.

2. After Armadillo asked Eagle for a bird's-eye view, Eagle

   _____.

3. After they finished their flight on the spaceship,

   _____.

With a partner, make a chart that tells the order in which Armadillo visited each place in the story. Display your chart in the classroom.

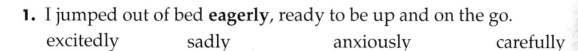

Name _____

Read the sentences. Underline the correct meaning for
the word in dark letters in each sentence.

1. I jumped out of bed **eagerly**, ready to be up and on the go.
   excitedly   sadly   anxiously   carefully

2. It was cold, but my hooded **parka** would keep me warm.
   blanket   automobile   jacket   rope

3. The moonlight on the snow looked **eerie**.
   boring   strange   bright   lost

4. I jumped into my **snowmobile** and started the engine.
   snow ski   snow shed   snow shovel   snow car

5. I remembered my father's stories about traveling on a
   sledge to go ice fishing.
   sled   carriage   truck   wheelbarrow

6. I was in a hurry, so I pushed the **throttle** all the way down.
   windshield wiper   gas lever   hand brake   door handle

7. I easily **maneuvered** the snowmobile around a pile of
   snow and shot straight across the frozen lake.
   moved   climbed   jumped   collapsed

Answer the riddle with one of the words in dark letters.

How do you describe an alien with twelve purple ears? _____

Name_____

Think about "The Secret of the Seal." Then
complete the summary chart below.

Story	Main Characters
The Secret of the Seal	Kyo and Uncle George

Kyo's Goal	Uncle George's Goal
Kyo wants to _____ _____ _____	Uncle George wants _____ _____ _____

Actions

What Kyo Does	What Uncle George Does
1. At night, Kyo _____ _____ _____	**2.** As a result, Uncle George follows _____ _____
3. Kyo tries to _____ _____	**4.** But Uncle George _____ _____
5. Kyo sings and _____ _____	

Outcomes for Kyo	Outcomes for Uncle George
_____ _____ _____	_____ _____ _____

Name _____

Read the paragraph and answer the questions about the underlined words.

   The Iditarod is a <u>dogsled</u> race. Teams of dogs pull each sled, or <u>sledge</u>, more than 1,000 miles. The dogsleds' <u>runners</u> glide across ice and snow. The dogs are <u>hitched</u> to the sled with leather straps, called a <u>harness</u>. Racers hold the long <u>traces</u>, or reins, and guide the dogs. They ride on the sleds or run alongside. Racers wear warm <u>parkas</u>, or coats. Each parka has a <u>hood</u> to keep the racer's head warm. Martin Buser holds the speed record in the Iditarod. He and his dogs finished it in just over 10 days in 1992.

1. There are two words in dogsled that help me figure out what

the word means. They are _____ and _____.

A dogsled is a _____.

2. A sledge is a _____.

3. The runners are the parts on a dogsled that _____.

I know that runners are probably not wheels because _____.

4. A harness is _____.

5. Reins are used with horses and wagons. In the same way, _____ are used with dogs and dogsleds.

6. A parka is _____.

7. Draw a parka's hood on a separate sheet of paper.

8. Draw a horse hitched to a wagon on a separate sheet of paper.

Name _____

A. Read the paragraph below. Underline the present-time verbs. The first one is done for you.

Gilbert looks everywhere for his turtle, Finny.
Gilbert's brothers help him. Finny walks very
slowly. Usually, he eats lettuce and pieces of apple
that Gilbert gives him. The brothers look in the yard.
They find Finny in the garden.

B. Complete each sentence by circling the correct form of the verb in parentheses ( ).

1. Seals (eat/eats) squid and fish.

2. Most seals (lives/live) along the coast.

3. The northern fur seal (spend/spends) the summer on the Aleutian Islands.

4. Soft fur (covers/cover) the body of a seal pup.

5. A seal (swim/swims) by using both its front and rear flippers.

What is your favorite kind of animal? Write two
sentences about the habits of this animal. Use
present-time verbs in your sentences.

_____

_____

•••

SUMMARIZING
the **L**EARNING   A present-time verb tells about action that happens

_____. To decide on the correct form of the verb, look at the _____.

Name _____

Read the story and answer the questions.

"Come on!" Utik yelled. "Let's play polar bear hunt!" Utik was very fit. He moved quickly, even on snowshoes.

Kusiq hurried to catch up. "Hey!" he yelled. "You're going toward the edge of the ice!"

"I'm not too close," said Utik. CRACK! That's when the ice he was standing on broke. Kusiq took off one snowshoe and held it out. "Grab it!" he screeched.

1. Which boy is more fit, Utik or Kusiq? _____ How do you know?

_____

2. Which boy is more daring? _____ How do you know? _____

_____

3. Which boy made an unwise decision? _____ How do you know?

_____

4. Which boy is a quick thinker? _____ How do you know? _____

_____

5. Which boy would you rather have for a friend? Why? _____

_____

SUMMARIZING
the **L**EARNING Sometimes an author tells what a character is like. Sometimes readers have to figure this out. To do that,

think about: _____ _____ .

Name _____

Look at the picture and read the caption. Then follow the directions.

Seals are handsome animals. Most seals live in the coldest parts of the world. They have flippers instead of arms and legs. The flippers make them strong swimmers. This seal's thick layer of fat helps the animal survive the cold winter. It also makes the seal look cuddly!

A. Write four facts about seals that you find in the picture and caption.

_____

_____

_____

_____

B. Write two opinions about seals. They can be from the picture caption above or opinions of your own.

_____

_____

_____

_____

Name _____

Read the story below. Draw a line under all the clue words that tell *when*. Then answer the questions.

A woodchuck lived in Sari's backyard. Sari called him Chuck and talked to him sometimes. In April, Chuck ate the lettuce plants. In May, he ate the bean plants. In June, he ate all the poppies.

"That's it!" said Sari's papa. That very day, he put a wire box in the yard. The next morning, the woodchuck was inside. Sari wanted to keep Chuck as a pet, but Papa said no. Just after breakfast, Sari and her papa let the woodchuck go in a wildlife refuge where he would have plenty to eat. That afternoon, Sari and her papa planted more poppies.

1. For how long did Chuck live in Sari's backyard? At least _____

2. How do you know? _____

3. When did Chuck eat the bean plants? _____

4. When did Chuck eat the poppies? _____

5. How long did it take to catch Chuck? _____

How do you know? _____

_____

6. What happened before Papa said "That's it!"? _____

7. What was the last thing that happened? _____

_____

Name _____

A. Read each sentence. Answer the question that follows it.

1. Deer migrated from the hills to our valley in search of water.
What birds do you think migrated south last winter?

_____

2. The grass had turned brown and dry in the drought.
How long might a drought last?

_____

3. The deer will browse on the grass.
What kinds of trees might giraffes browse on?

_____

4. With a sharp tool, we pierced some wooden beads.
What would happen if you pierced a balloon?

_____

5. The beads were strung on string.
How will birds get the popcorn that was strung on the tree?

_____

6. The rain is overdue. I hope the rain will not be so
belated that the deer will not survive.
When would you receive a belated birthday card?

_____

B. Use each word in a sentence of your own.

1. pierced _____

2. browse _____

3. drought _____

4. migrated _____

Name _____

Think about what happened in the story "Bringing the Rain to Kapiti Plain." Complete this story frame below. If you need to, cross out your predictions and write new answers.

This story takes place _____.

The problem in the story is _____

_____.

Ki-pat gets an idea for ending the drought when _____

_____.

The drought is ended when _____

_____.

At the ending of the story, _____

_____.

Imagine that a friend has asked you what this story is about. Write what you would say in one sentence.

_____

_____

Name _____

Draw a picture for each word to show a different
meaning. Then write a sentence using the word pair.
The first one has been done for you.

close (near)

close (shut)

If you are close to the door, please close it. _____

tear (rip)	**tear (teardrop)**

stair	**stare**

pair	**pear**

Name _____

A. Read the paragraph below. Underline the past-time verbs. Circle the ending in each one.

Last summer I visited my cousin's farm. Every morning I helped feed their cows and pigs. I enjoyed working with animals. While my cousin and I worked, my aunt cooked a big breakfast. I liked to smell the bacon and eggs as I walked through the door.

B. Change the verb in parentheses ( ) to tell about the past, and then write it in the blank.

1. Last year it (rain) _____ on my birthday.

2. We (move) _____ all the party tables and chairs into the house.

3. I (open) _____ my presents after we had cake and ice cream.

Write a sentence about something that happened to you in the past. Use a past-time verb.

_____

_____

• •

SUMMARIZING
the **L**EARNING   A verb that shows action that happened in the past is called

a _____. Add _____ or _____ to most present-time

verbs to make them show past time.

Name _____

Read the paragraph and think about what happens.
Then answer the questions.

It had not rained for weeks. All the gardens were brown and
dead. Where once there was green grass, there was only dust.
Then a cloud passed over the sun, and another cloud. A sound
began on the roofs. *Pitter-patter, pitter-patter, pitter-patter.* All
the people ran outside. "Hurray!" they yelled.

1. Why were the gardens brown and dead? _____ .
How do you know?
    The story tells me _____ .

    And I already know that _____ .

2. What was the sound on the roof? _____
How do you know? (Give two examples.)

    The story says _____ .

    I know that _____ .

    The story says _____ .

    I know that _____ .

3. How did the people feel when they heard the sound? _____
How do you know?

    The story says _____ .

    I know that _____ .

SUMMARIZING
the **L**EARNING   Write how you draw a conclusion:

Evidence from _____ + _____ = Conclusion

Name_____

Read the story. Think about the meanings of the underlined words. Then write each word in the box where it belongs.

When I was a child, I wanted to be a fire fighter. I could picture myself parachuting out of planes. I would fight the flames until they smoldered and died out. I would stop fire from consuming trees and grassy meadows. I wanted all the trees to live and grow, not die as fuel for fires. Now I am older and I know that saving the forests takes science as well as fire fighters. Each forest is a complete ecosystem of natural things living together. We have to understand what nutrients plants need to live. We need to study the repeating cycles in nature of how trees die and grow back again and again. I still want to save the trees, but now I want to be a forest ranger.

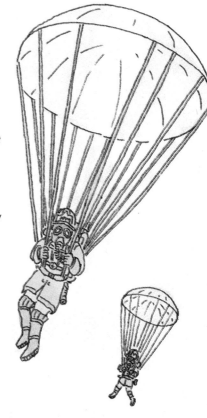

<table>
<tr><td>

1. circles   wheels

_____
</td><td>

2. food   minerals

_____
</td><td>

3. plants + animals + place =

_____
</td></tr>
<tr><td>

4. died out   smoked

_____
</td><td>

5. flying   jumping floating

_____
</td><td>

6. eating   using up

_____
</td></tr>
</table>

7.   burning +

    _____ = energy

Name_____

Use the **KWL** chart to help you read "Flames and Rebirth." Write in the first two columns before you read. Add to the second column during reading. Fill in the last column after you read the selection.

K	W	L
What I Know	**What I Want to Know**	**What I Learned**

The most important thing I learned in this story is _____

_____.

Name _____

Read the glossary page below. Then answer the
questions and fill in the blanks.

---

canopy fire   **plant**

canopy fire [kan′ə•pē fīr] *n.* A
    fire in the living tops of trees

cycle [sī′kəl]*n.* Events that
    happen in the same order, over
    and over again

ecosystem [ek′ ō•sis′ təm] *n.* The
    living things and the land in
    one particular place

firebrand [fīr′ brand′] *n.* A piece
    of burning material, such as a
    pine cone, carried by the wind

lodgepole pine [läj′ pōl pīn] *n.* A
    type of fast-growing evergreen
    tree

nutrient [n(y)o͞o′ trē•ənt] *n.* The
    useful part of food

---

1. What are the guide words on this glossary page? _____

2. How can guide words be useful?

    _____

3. What entry word begins with the same sound as *simple* and *sudden*? _____

4. What are three *nutrients* for people?

    _____

5. A(n) _____ can spread a forest fire on a windy day.

6. Use the words in parentheses ( ) in sentences.

    (canopy fire) _____

    _____

    (cycle) _____

    _____

Name _____

A. Read the following paragraph. Circle the irregular past-time verbs.

Two years ago my family and I went to Yellowstone National Park. We drove all the way from California. My best friend, Robbie, came with us. He ate too many cookies on the way there. They gave him a stomachache.

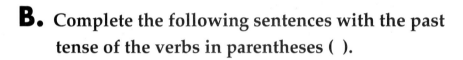

B. Complete the following sentences with the past tense of the verbs in parentheses ( ).

1. Yuen and her family (go) _____ camping last summer.

2. They (drive) _____ to a ranger station near a burnt-out forest.

3. At noon, they (take) _____ a break to eat lunch.

4. After they (eat) _____ lunch, everyone helped put out the campfire.

Write two sentences about something exciting that happened to you during a trip outdoors. Use two past-time verbs from the sentences above.

_____

_____

•••

SUMMARIZING *the* **L**EARNING   A verb that does not end with *-ed* to show past time is

called an _____ verb.

Name _____

Read the paragraph and think about likenesses and differences. Then complete the page.

My family was going to camp out at Yellowstone National Park. We couldn't decide which campsite was better, number 16 or number 21. Both campsites were the same distance from the river. Number 16 got a lot more sun, which was nice. My mom liked 16 better because it had a view of the mountains. Dad liked 21 better. It didn't have a view, but it was in the trees, so we could put up our hammock. Both campsites were nice and big. Which one would you choose?

Name two things that are the same about the campsites.

1. _____

2. _____

Name three things that are different about the campsites.

3. _____

4. _____

5. _____

6. Which campsite would you use? _____

SUMMARIZING
the **L**EARNING   Noticing how things are *alike* or *different* can help me understand what I am reading better. The word *both* is

a clue word used when two things are —————. The words *more* and *less*

are clue words used when two things are _____.

Name _____

Read each paragraph and the summaries that follow it.
Fill in the circle beside the better summary. Then
explain your choice on the line below it.

A little room perched on a tower high in the mountains. Its
windows looked out over miles of forest. In the room lived a
fire ranger. It was her job to be on the lookout for smoke. To
avoid disasters, it was important to spot fires when they first
started. Rarely did the ranger see anyone. Food supplies were
trucked in once a week.

○ The fire ranger didn't have a lot to do. Her room was high in the

mountains.

○ The fire ranger had an important and lonely job. She lived in a little room

high in the mountains and watched for smoke.

_____

Tim was in firefighters' school. He had to climb down a ladder
carrying a heavy pack over his shoulder. At first, Tim became
very frightened. He felt as if he couldn't move. Then he imagined
it was a real boy he was carrying. He knew he had to get the
child out of the smoke. He climbed down with no trouble.

○ Tim can carry a child down a big firefighter's ladder.

○ Tim got over his fear by imagining he was
carrying a real child down the ladder.

_____

SUMMARIZING
the **L**EARNING   A _____ is short and tells only the most
important ideas.

Name _____

Many libraries now use computerized card catalogs, or data bases. Suppose you follow instructions on the computer to find books about forest fires. You look up forest fires, and you might then see a screen like the one below. Use it to answer the questions that follow.

```
CALL # 634.9

AUTHOR: VOGEL, CAROLE GARBUNY, AND
KATHRYN ALLEN GOLDNER

TITLE: GREAT YELLOWSTONE FIRE, THE

PUBLISHER: NEW YORK: LITTLE, BROWN, 1990

LOCATION: MAIN LIBRARY, QUEENS BRANCH
LIBRARY
21 LISTED AT MAIN LIBRARY. PRESS <RETURN>
TO SEE MORE, OR TYPE: HELP, THEN PRESS
<RETURN>
```

1. What is the name of the book found by the computer? _____

_____

2. What libraries have the book? _____

3. If you went to the library shelves, how would you find the book? _____

_____

4. You want to find more books about forest fires. What would you do next on

the computer? _____

5. Suppose you are not sure what to do next. To get help from the computer,

what would you do? _____

Name _____

Read the paragraphs. Write three details and the main idea for each.

Conditions in Yellowstone National Park were just right for fires in 1988. Trees had been growing and dying there for two hundred years. Dead wood littered the ground. Little rain or snow had fallen all year. It was the driest summer ever in the park.

Detail _____

Detail _____

Detail _____

Main Idea _____

_____

Wind carries firebrands through the air to spread the fire. It helps fires leap small streams and other natural firebreaks. Of course, wind helps fire race with frightening speed across the land, too. Then firefighting is especially difficult and dangerous.

Detail _____

Detail _____

Detail _____

Main Idea _____

Name _____

Read the story. Think about the meanings of the
underlined words. Then use each word in a sentence of
your own.

   My grandma told great stories. We loved the different
ways she told "Little Red Riding Hood." The wolf was
always so tricky and <u>cunning</u>! The <u>route</u> through the
woods to her Grandma's house was so dark and spooky!
Red Riding Hood was <u>plump</u> because she ate so many
biscuits with honey. Once the wolf <u>disguised</u> himself as
a bottled-water salesman. Another time he ran after poor
Red with an <u>awl</u>. He said he wanted to repair her shoes.
"No! No! Don't trust him, Red!" my sister and I would
yell. We shivered and <u>embraced</u> each other in a big
hug. When it was time to go to bed, we made sure to
<u>latch</u> the back door. Even though we were frightened
for a while, we knew we were safe.

1. cunning _____.

2. route _____.

3. plump _____.

4. disguised _____.

5. awl _____.

6. embraced _____.

7. latch _____.

••• LON PO PO •••

Name _____

Complete this story map to tell what
happened in the story.

Title	Setting
Lon Po Po	China

Characters

mother, Shang, Tao, Paotze, wolf

Problem

_____

What happens

1. _____

2. _____

3. _____

4. _____

Solution

_____

_____

Name _____

A. Read the following paragraph. Underline all the past-time verbs. Circle the irregular past-time verbs.

Yesterday I rode to my grandmother's house on my bike. I ran up the porch steps. Then I saw Grandma. She saw me through the window. She ran to the front door to let me in. "I had an idea you might visit today," she said. "I baked some cookies because I thought you would enjoy them."

B. Complete each sentence by circling the correct verb in parentheses ( ).

1. I (had/have) lots of homework to do last night.

2. While I was studying, I (think/thought) I heard a knock at the front door.

3. "Who could that be?" I (says/said) to myself.

4. It was my friend Sonia, who had (ride/ridden) to my house on her bike.

Write a sentence about a clever thing you have done.
Use at least one irregular past-time verb.

_____

_____

SUMMARIZING
the **L**EARNING   Some irregular past-time verbs are _____,

_____, and _____.

Name _____

Read the paragraphs below. Draw a line under all the words that are spoken. Then answer the questions.

An old man was making a basket. "Mei Hua," he said, "next month is Liang's birthday."

"Yes, Hoy," said Mei Hua. "I will bake special moon cakes."

"We must have a special gift for such a special grandson. I think it is time for his first bicycle."

"But, my husband," said Mei Hua. "A bicycle will cost so much! And we will have to travel all the way to the city to find one!"

"I will sell some baskets," Hoy said. "We can go to the city together and have some fun!" He kissed the old woman's cheek.

1. What are the names of the characters speaking? _____

2. How are they related? _____

3. How do you know? _____

4. Who is Liang? _____

5. How does Hoy feel about Liang? _____

_____

How do you know? _____

_____

6. Where do the characters live? _____

How do you know? _____

_____

Name_____

Read the paragraph, and then compare and contrast the girls. On the left side, write things that describe just Lee. On the right side, write things that describe just Lien. In the middle, write things that describe both girls.

Lee and Lien are twin sisters. They both have thick black hair and pretty, round faces. They are both exactly four feet tall. They both have double-jointed toes. But looks aren't everything! Lee loves computer games. She plays with friends for hours, and she always wins. Computers bore Lien. She likes to play outside. Lien makes beautiful kites from balsa wood and paper. On sunny days, she is always outside flying them. The girls' grandfather says they are twins on the outside, but not on the inside!

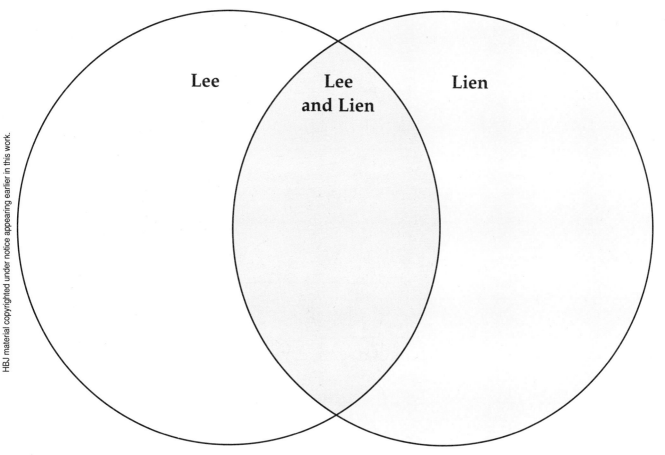

Lee   Lee
             and Lien   Lien

Name _____

Read about these meetings between grandparents and
grandchildren. Use what you read and what you already
know to answer the questions.

Grandma was lying in a bed so high that Millie had to
stand on tiptoe to kiss her cheek. There were two other
empty beds in the room. There was a buzzer that said
NURSE on it. Grandma looked pale and tired. "I brought
you some flowers, Grandma," Millie said.

1. Where are Millie and Grandma? _____

2. How do you know? _____

_____

3. How does Millie feel about her grandmother? _____

4. How do you know? _____

As soon as Terry saw the red car pull up, he
raced outside. "Grandpa! Grandpa!" he yelled.
When the car door opened, Terry threw himself
into his grandfather's arms.

5. How does Terry feel about his grandfather? _____

_____

How do you know? _____

_____

6. Do you think Terry sees his grandfather every day? _____

Why do you think so? I know that people _____

_____

Name _____

A. Read the sentences. Draw a line under the correct meaning for the word in dark letters in each sentence.

1. Suzy is our **agent** in charge of missing persons.

   hired helper   dentist   agreement   actor

2. It's just an after-school job, but it helps her parents pay for their big **penthouse**.

   penny   friendship   apartment at the top   money paid
                            of a building   for work done

3. A **chauffeur** in a big car takes Suzy where she wants to go.

   cleaner   driver   cheater   helper

4. Herbert Hoover School is one **client** that hired Suzy.

   clerk   clip   customer   class

5. Once she found the principal's missing salad, but the lettuce was **limp**.

   long   droopy   broken   stiff

B. Fill out the form. Use each word in parentheses ( ) in a sentence.

SMART EYE INVESTIGATIONS
Found Person Report

Name of Suspect _Clarence Hardy, also known as "Tardy" Hardy_ ___

Problem _Mr. Hardy was late for school...AGAIN!_ ___

Description (limp) _____

Last Seen (penthouse) _____

Witness Statement (chauffeur) _____

Job Description (client) _____

Steps Taken and Outcome (agent) _____

THE PIZZA MONSTER

Name ________________________________

Complete the prediction chart below. Use it to retell the story "The Pizza Monster."

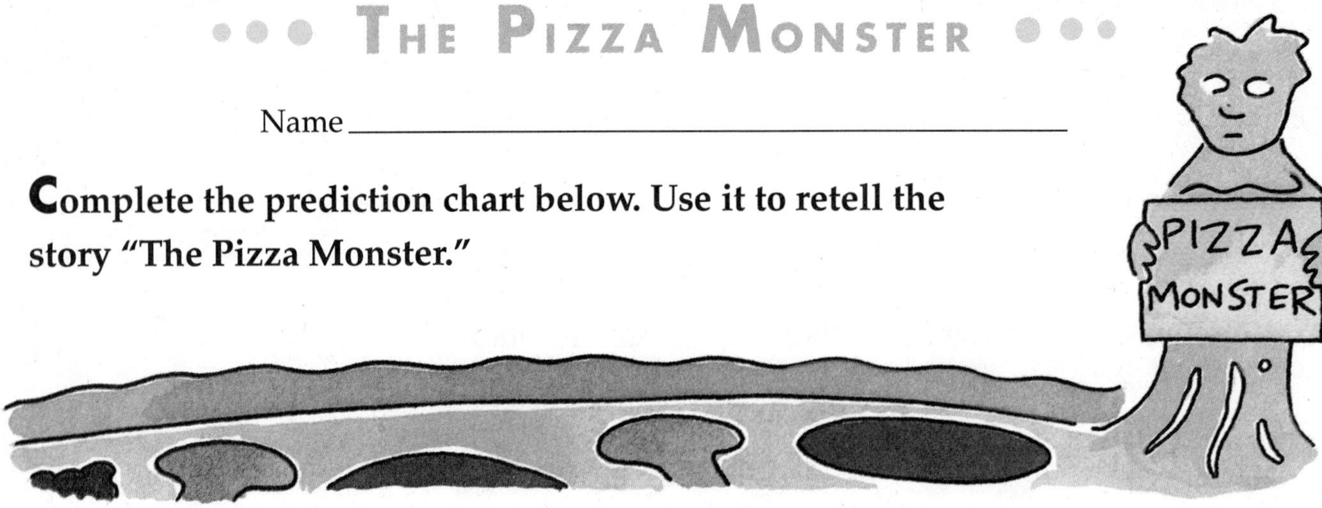

	What I Predict	What Happened
Think about the main character.		
Think about the title.		
Think about the story ending.		

Write what happened in one sentence.

____

____

____

Name _____

A. Imagine that you are a detective, like Olivia. Think of words that describe a good detective. Add them to the web.

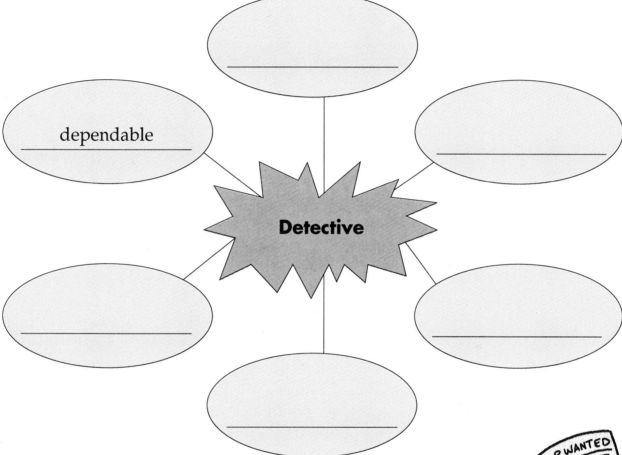

dependable

Detective

B. Now write an advertisement. Try to persuade people to hire you. Use some of the words from your web. Don't forget your name and phone number.

_____

_____

_____

_____

Name _____

A. Circle the forms of the verb *be*.

I was upset yesterday when I lost my lucky eraser. "It is only an eraser," said my father. "But this eraser was my lucky eraser!" I shouted as I ran to my room. When I got there, I noticed that my pet parakeet Clancy had something in his beak. It was my eraser! "So you are the thief!" I said.

B. Complete each sentence by circling the correct word in parentheses ( ).

1. I (are/am) a good detective.

2. If you (is/are) in trouble, I (am/is) the person that can help you.

3. Once my little sister (were/was) frightened because she thought monsters lived under her bed.

4. "If they (am/are) here," I told her, "we'll find them."

5. I showed her that nothing (was/were) there.

••

SUMMARIZING *the* **L**EARNING   *Am, are, is, was,* and _____ are forms of the verb

_____. _____ and _____ are used with a singular subject.

Are and *were* are used with _____ subjects and with _____.

Name _____

A. Imagine that you are a detective, like Olivia in "The Pizza Monster." Rosa has lost her dog. Read what she has to say. Take notes on the important ideas and details. Write them on the note pad.

My name is Rosa Torres, and my dog's name is Honeybunch. I just don't know where she could be! I'm so worried!

We live at 44 Market Street, Newtown, California. It's a big blue house with a fence around it. My phone number is 555-6699.

Honeybunch is the cutest dog! She is a basset hound, dark brown and white. She has a yellow collar with my phone number on it.

I was going to take her to the vet for her shots on Saturday morning. That was April 2. She just wasn't in the backyard! I couldn't find a hole in the fence or anything, though.

She's a friendly dog, and she comes when you call her name. She loves popcorn, so if she doesn't want to come to me, I just hold some popcorn out.

GO ON

The only place I can think of where my dog might have gone on her own is our old house. We moved three weeks ago. We used to live at the corner of Elm and Birch streets. But that's more than four miles away! I miss my dog so much! Please help me!

_____

_____

_____

_____

_____

B. Now pick out the key words and ideas from your notes. Write them on this note card so you can have all the information with you while you search for Honeybunch.

Client _____   Phone _____

_____

_____

Problem _____

Description _____

_____

Last seen _____

Places to look _____

How to catch _____

_____

Name_____

Read about the pizzas and answer the questions.

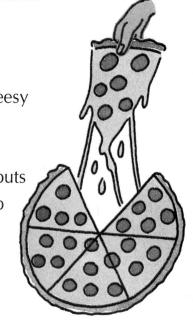

Where should we buy our pizza? Both Ed's Pizza and Cheesy Pizza make good ones. They both have thick crust, which I like. Ed's tomato sauce is more spicy. Do you like lots of cheese? Cheesy Pizza is cheesier than Ed's. Still, I think Ed puts on more pepperoni. Ed delivers, but we will have to pick up our own pizza if we order it from Cheesy. Both pizzas are about the same size. So, should I call Ed's or Cheesy?

In what three ways are Ed's Pizza and Cheesy Pizza alike?

1. _____

2. _____

3. _____

In what four ways are Ed's Pizza and Cheesy Pizza different?

4. _____

5. _____

6. _____

7. _____

Where would you buy your pizza? Why? _____

_____

THE PIZZA MONSTER

Name _____

Read the paragraphs and think about what happened.
Be a detective and answer the questions.

When I got home, I looked in the goldfish bowl. One fish
was missing. My three cats—Huey, Dewey, and Louie—
were sitting near the bowl. They looked completely
innocent.

"Here, kitties," I called. The cats came to me, and Dewey
left wet paw prints all across the floor.

"Dewey, what have you done?" I scolded.

1. What happened to the missing goldfish? _____
   How do you know?

   The story tells me that _____.

   I already know that cats _____.

When the baby-sitter got back to the kitchen, there was
maple syrup everywhere. It dripped on the table, the
dishes, and the floor. The baby-sitter looked at the triplets.

"Okay," she said. "I want each of you to get a paper
towel and bring it to me so I can clean up this mess." Pam,
Sam, and Tam got paper towels. But when Pam tried to
hand hers over, it stuck to her fingers.

2. Who made the mess? _____
   How do you know?

   The story tells me that _____.

   I already know that maple syrup _____.

Name _____

Finish the quilt by writing each word in the square where it belongs. The words you will need are below.

| last | faded | textures | patchwork | worn | masterpiece |

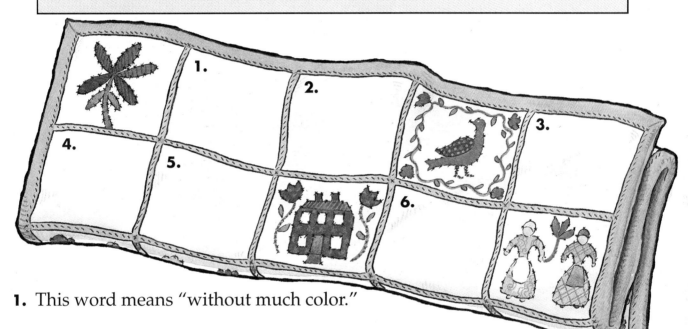

1. This word means "without much color."

2. This word means "the greatest thing a person has ever done."

3. This word describes a quilt that is made from pieces of different kinds of cloth.

4. This word means "much used."

5. "Smooth" and "bumpy" describe different _____.

6. This word means "stay" or "not disappear."

ACTIVITY CORNER

With a group, make a bulletin board display about quilting. Use drawings, captions, and pieces of cloth to explain how quilts are made. Include some of the vocabulary words in your captions.

••• THE PATCHWORK QUILT •••

Name _____

Complete the story map to tell what happens in "The Patchwork Quilt."

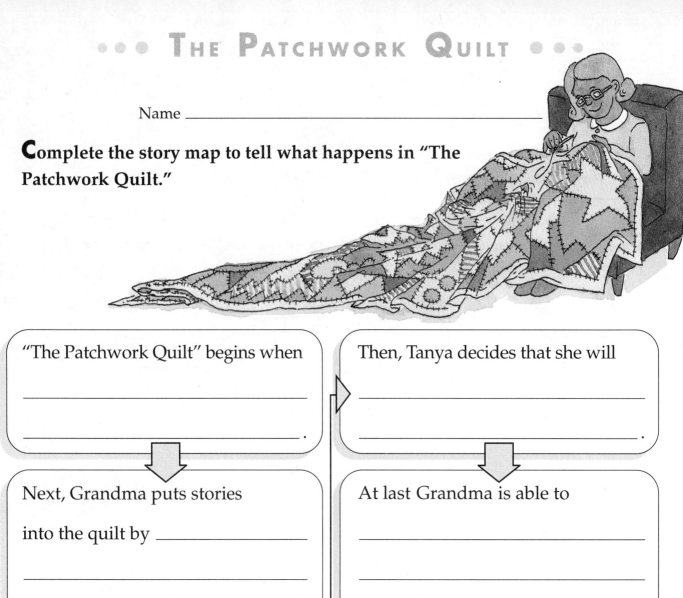

"The Patchwork Quilt" begins when
_____
_____ .

Next, Grandma puts stories

into the quilt by _____
_____
_____ .

Then, Grandma stops working

on the quilt when _____
_____
_____ .

Then, Tanya decides that she will
_____
_____ .

At last Grandma is able to
_____
_____ .

Finally, the quilt is finished. The

family is proud of it because
_____
_____ .

Reading this story made me feel _____
_____ .

HBJ material copyrighted under notice appearing earlier in this work.

Name _____

A. Read the paragraph below. Circle the adverb that describes each underlined verb. Look for a word that tells *how, when,* or *where* the action happens.

Sometimes my grandmother visits us. She often brings her knitting with her. Grandma sits upstairs in my room. She works slowly. Someday she will teach me to knit.

B. Choose the adverb from the box that best fits in each blank below. Use the clues in parentheses ( ) to help you.

often	carefully	cleverly	downstairs

My grandmother is also a woodcarver. She keeps her tools

_____ in the basement. She _____ works on
(Where?)   (When?)

her carving after we eat dinner. With a carving tool in hand, she

_____ cuts the wood. After a week or two, she has
(How?)

_____ carved something beautiful.
(How?)

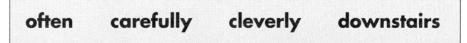

SUMMARIZING
the **L**EARNING   An adverb is a word that describes a _____. An adverb

may tell _____, _____, or _____ an action happens.

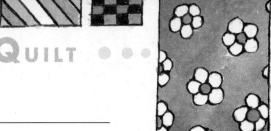

THE PATCHWORK QUILT

Name _____

A. Read the first paragraph, which tells about the quilt.

> Grandma spent many hours working on her quilt. The scraps of cloth she sewed into the quilt reminded her of people and events from the past. "A quilt can tell a story," she said.

Now read this paraphrase and answer the questions below.

> Grandma worked hard on her quilt. She believed a quilt told stories, because the materials in the quilt made her think of people and events.

Is this a good paraphrase of the paragraph? _____

Why or why not? _____

B. Rewrite these sayings in your own words.

1. A penny saved is a penny earned.

_____

2. A stitch in time saves nine.

_____

Think of several famous sayings like the ones above. Write each saying in your own words on a square of paper. Tape your squares together with your classmates' squares to make a paper quilt.

Name_____

Read each sentence carefully. Think about the word or words that the pronoun in parentheses ( ) replaces. Write that word or words on the line.

1. Grandma was very proud of her quilt. (She) _____ called it her masterpiece.

2. Jim really liked his blue pants. He didn't want to stop

   wearing (them) _____ even when they were worn out.

3. Grandma called to Jim. Then (he) _____ watched as she cut some squares from the pants.

4. When Grandma became ill, Tanya was sad. (She)

   _____ missed watching Grandma work on

   the quilt.

5. Mom, Tanya, Jim, and Ted started to work on the quilt. (They)

   _____ all wanted to finish it.

6. When the quilt was done, Tanya held (it) _____ up.

7. Papa looked at Tanya. Papa said that (she) _____ had done a wonderful job.

Name_____

A. Read the words and their meanings. Then write each word in the group where it belongs.

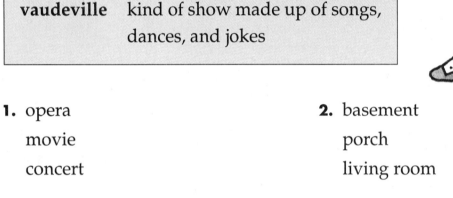

attic	space at the top of a house
finale	the last act in a show
glances	looks quickly
vaudeville	kind of show made up of songs, dances, and jokes

1. opera
movie
concert

_____

2. basement
porch
living room

_____

3. end
closing
curtains

_____

4. stares
peeks
looks

_____

B. Use each word in a sentence of your own.

attic _____

finale _____

glances _____

vaudeville _____

Name _____

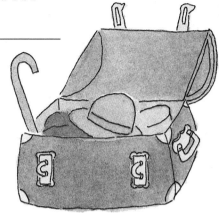

Before you read the story "Song and Dance Man," look at the title, the illustrations, and the first few sentences. Write what you predict will happen. After you read the story, write what really happens.

What I Predict Will Happen	What Really Happens

"Song and Dance Man" is a good title for this story

because _____

_____ .

Name_____

A. Read the paragraph below. Then find the meaning of each underlined word. Write the number of that meaning on the line next to the word. The first one is done for you.

1. also	**4.** you are
2. the number 2	**5.** belonging to you
3. in the direction of	

We explored your __5__ attic yesterday. I found two _____ Western

hats and a pair of boots. Your sister found some boots, too. _____ We

pretended we were on a trip to _____ a cattle ranch. You're _____ lucky

that your attic is filled with so many wonderful things!

B. Write the correct word in parentheses ( ) on the line.

1. " (You're/Your) _____ a song and dance man," said Maria.

2. "I don't often go (too/to) _____ the theater anymore," Bill
said sadly.

3. "I have (two/too) _____ tickets," Maria said with a smile.

••

SUMMARIZING
the **LEARNING**   Use _____ when you mean "in the direction of." Use

_____ when you mean "also." Use _____ when you mean the

number 2. Use _____ when you mean "belonging to you." Use

_____ when you mean "you are."

Name_____

Read the story and then follow the directions below.

(a) The third-grade class show was a big hit with the parents, thanks to Evan. Evan played a farmer, and his best friend Wendy was a sunflower. Wendy sang a song. Then she was supposed to dance off the stage. (b) Instead, she just stood there like a tree trunk, her face getting redder and redder. Suddenly, Evan saw what was wrong. The stem on Wendy's flower costume had slipped, and she couldn't move her legs an inch! (c) Evan, who is a quick thinker, saved the day. He said it was time to pick the sunflower. Then he helped Wendy into his wheelbarrow and wheeled her off the stage.

Write a summary of the story. Use only one or two sentences.

_____

_____

_____

Paraphrase sections (a), (b), and (c).

(a) _____

(b) _____

(c) _____

Name _____

Each sentence below uses a simile or a metaphor. Draw
a line under the two things being compared. Then write
a new sentence that means the same thing but does not
use figurative language.

1. I was a tap-dancing machine when I was practicing for

the show. _____

2. But the truth is, I was a chicken about performing in the show.

_____

3. I knew my dancing was as graceful as an elephant stampede.

_____

4. Luckily, my dance teacher was as smart as a fox.

_____

5. She also had a heart as big as a dance hall.

_____

6. She gave me a costume that looked like a big, gray quilt.

_____

7. That elephant costume was a lifesaver.

_____

8. Now I could dance like an elephant and not be embarrassed!

_____

Name _____

Read about the two attics and then follow the directions.

It is a rainy day, and we can't decide where to play. Should we go to Randall's attic? It is used for storage. It is neat and clean, with everything packed in boxes. There's lots of bare space for dancing and putting on shows. Or should we play in Leslie's attic? It is used for storage, too, but everything is spread around. There is barely room to move, with all the old clothes and toys lying around. Both attics are fun to play in. Where should we go?

1. Write two ways the attics are alike.

_____

_____

2. Write three ways the attics are different.

_____

_____

_____

3. Which attic would you rather play in? _____

4. Imagine the attics. Write two sentences. Show one more way they may be alike and one more way they may be different.

Alike _____

Different _____

Name _____

Read the sentences. Draw a line under the correct meaning for the word in dark letters in each sentence.

1. We found some very old **documents** written in Spanish.
   dollars   papers   domes   piers

2. They were sealed in wax, which **preserves** paper for a time.
   burns   cooks   saves   writes

3. Luckily, Mr. Garcia could **translate** the words into English.
   restate   rewrite   review   reappear

4. They told about a Spanish **galleon**, sailing in a storm.
   flying kite   moving van   selling booth   sailing ship

5. The ship hit an underwater **reef** and sank near Spain.
   ledge   fish   hose   chimney

6. It was carrying silver and gold coins as its **cargo!**
   lesson   payment   fuel   load

7. If the **salvage** goes well, we will be rich!
   recovery of goods   ruined property   new clothes   wasted time

8. If we can get money from some **investors**, the treasure hunt will begin!
   helpers   thieves   tailors   lenders

Name_____

Complete this **KWL** chart to help you read "Sunken Treasure." Write in the first two parts before you read. Add to the second column during reading. Fill in the last part after you read.

K	**W**	**L**
What I Know	*What I Want to Know*	*What I Learned*

The most important thing I learned in this story is _____

_____.

Name_____

A. Add the prefix *dis-*, meaning "not," or *re-*, meaning "again," to each underlined word. Make a new word that fits in the sentence.

1. Ancient sailors _____ about the shape of the earth.
   (the opposite of <u>agreed</u>)

2. Many thought ships could drop off the earth and _____.
   (the opposite of <u>appear</u>)

3. They _____ of ships sailing too far into unknown waters.
   (the opposite of <u>approved</u>)

4. They felt safer just _____ their old routes.
   (<u>tracing</u> again)

5. Then people learned that the earth was round, and old

   maps had to be _____.
   (<u>drawn</u> again)

B. Draw a line under the prefixes. Then complete each sentence in your own words.

1. If I disobey my parents, _____

   _____.

2. I had to repack everything because _____

   _____.

3. I distrust Sally because she _____

   _____.

4. To repatch the sail, I will _____

   _____.

Name_____

A. Complete each sentence. Write a word from the box
in each blank space. Remember to capitalize the
first word in a sentence.

| its | it's | their | there | they're |

_____ dark beneath the water's surface.

The divers use _____ lights to see into the ship.

When they find a treasure chest, _____ very excited.

The chest is closed, but _____ latch is broken.

_____, inside the chest, the divers find many jewels.

B. Write two sentences describing where or how you
might look for sunken treasure. Use two of the
words from the box above in your sentences.

_____

_____

_____

· ·

SUMMARIZING
the **L**EARNING   Use _____ when you mean "belonging to it." Use

_____ when you mean "it is." Use _____ when you mean

"belonging to them." Use _____ when you mean "in that place." Use

_____ when you mean "they are."

Name _____

A. Read what each part of the SQ3R strategy means.

S	Survey (Look at headings, pictures, and organization.)	3R	Read
			Recite (Say an oral summary.)
Q	Question		Review (Look back and answer the questions.)

B. Survey the story below. Answer the questions.

TREASURE IN THE DESERT

At the bottom of the sea or under desert sands, wherever there are rumors of treasure, you will find treasure hunters. One of the greatest treasures of all time was found in the sands of Egypt.

King Tut

Tutankhamen (Tut) was a king, or *pharaoh*, in Egypt 3,000 years ago. He ruled from age 9 until he was 18. He ordered that a great treasure be buried with him when he died. The burial place was secret. King Tut didn't want robbers to find his treasure. He believed in life after death, and he wanted all his precious things with him.

The Treasure Hunt

Most people thought that all the Egyptian kings' tombs had been found. They were wrong. A man named Howard Carter had studied Egypt. He believed that King Tut's treasure was still hidden. He was right, but it took him and an explorer friend five years of digging to find it.

GO ON

Name _____

The Treasure

Tut's treasure, found many years ago, was amazing. It included gold thrones, chariots, jewelry, statues, weapons, and a gold mask of the **Pharaoh** himself. It took ten years to empty the tomb of its treasure.

Its Importance

All the things in Tut's tomb helped scientists see what life was like in ancient Egypt. They told many secrets from ancient times.

1. What headings tell what the story is about? Draw a line under them.

2. What is one new word the writer thinks is important? _____

   How do you know? _____

3. Write questions you would ask about this story before reading.
   (Questions ask who, where, what, why, how, when.)

   _____   _____

   _____   _____

   _____   _____

C. Read the story.

D. Tell what you would do after reading to study the story.

   _____

   _____

   _____

   _____

Name_____

Read the paragraph and study the diagram. Use what you have learned to answer the questions.

**Spanish Galleon
early 1600s**

main mast

foremast

lateen
sail

poop

sterncastle

quarter deck

stern

bow

bulwarks

Galleons served as warships and cargo ships in the 1600s. These ships used square sails on their foremasts and mainmasts. Masts near the rear of the ship used lateen sails. Galleons had high decks called poops in their sterns. The bulwarks of galleons were three to four feet thick in case of attack. Still, Spanish galleons became a favorite target of pirates. The ships were slow and hard to turn. And they were often used to carry gold and silver from the New World.

GO ON

Name _____

1. Where is the stern of a ship? _____

2. What is a mast? _____

3. Which mast is the quarterdeck near? _____

4. Living quarters were in the sterncastle. Where is that?

   _____

5. Which deck is above the sterncastle? _____

6. Why did pirates attack Spanish galleons?

   a. _____

   b. _____

7. What are bulwarks? _____

8. Draw a square sail.   Draw a lateen sail.

9. How are the two sails different? _____

   _____

Name_____

A. **Read the paragraph and think about the main points.**

Philip and his family spent their summer vacation on an island. Philip played on the beach from morning to night. He imagined he was Philip the Brave, a pirate who built a sand hideout. He imagined he was a track star and ran as fast as he could on the sand. He swam and dove like a dolphin in the blue water. One day, while Philip was building a sand castle, he found something in the sand. It was an old Spanish coin!

Now read these postcards and answer the questions.

1. Philip, who can swim well, found Spanish treasure that washed ashore from a sunken ship.

Is this a good summary of the paragraph? _____ Why or why not? _____

_____

_____

2. While he was on vacation, Philip played many pretend games and even found a Spanish coin on the beach.

Is this a good summary of the paragraph? _____ Why or why not?

_____

_____

_____

Name_____

B. **Write a paraphrase of each sentence on the postcard below it.**

1. Philip spent many hours building a sand castle on the beach, and he was sad when the waves washed it away.

2. Even when the weather was cool and rainy, Philip played on the beach all day.

Read a library book about diving or searching for sunken treasure. Write a short summary of what you've read. Share your summary with your classmates.

Name _____

Read the words in the box and think about their meanings. Then complete the sentences by writing each word where it belongs.

timbers	wood for building boats	**towing**	pulling by a rope or a chain
ominous	threatening		
port	place where ships may arrive and depart	**tiller**	bar used to steer a boat
		harbor	place where ships may anchor and be safe
cockpit	open space on the deck of a boat where a person can steer		

1. The sailboat's frame is made of wooden _____.

2. A tugboat is used for _____ other boats.

3. The dark clouds look _____. No sailing today!

4. The water in the _____ is calm.

5. The person steering the boat sits in the _____.

6. Instead of a steering wheel, the boat has a _____.

7. Just a few small boats dock at this _____.

Name_____

Think about the story "The Wreck of the *Zephyr.*" Write
in the chart the main things that happened. Check *Fact* or
Fantasy for each one. The first one has been done for you.

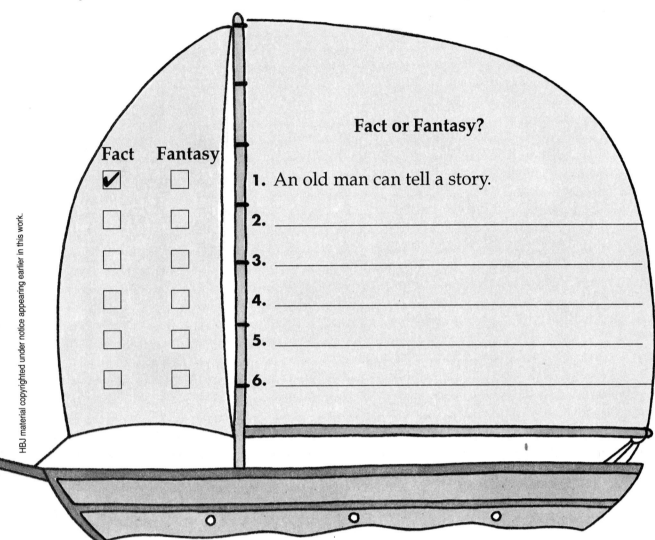

Fact or Fantasy?

Fact   Fantasy

☑ ☐ **1.** An old man can tell a story.

☐ ☐ **2.** _____

☐ ☐ **3.** _____

☐ ☐ **4.** _____

☐ ☐ **5.** _____

☐ ☐ **6.** _____

Write what happens in the story in one sentence.

In this fantasy, _____

_____.

Name _____

Add the prefix *un-,* meaning "not," or the suffix *-er* or *-or,* meaning "one who," to the underlined base word. Write the new word in the blank. Then complete the sentence in your own words. (One has been done for you.)

1. The <u>usual</u> place to see a boat is on the water.

It would be ___unusual___ to see ___a boat flying in the air___.

2. I would like to <u>sail</u> my own little boat on the sea.

If I were a _____ , I would _____

_____.

3. My boat needed a new coat of <u>paint</u> badly.

I hired a _____ , who _____

_____.

4. My grandfather knew all about <u>safe</u> sailing.

He said it was _____ to sail _____

_____.

5. It is a hard job to <u>build</u> a boat.

The _____ must know _____

_____.

Name_____

A. Read the dialogue below. Circle all the commas that set off introductory words. Underline each comma that sets off an item in a series.

Sailor: We had an exciting time on the sailboat today. The sky was filled with clouds, rain, and a lot of wind.
Reporter: What happened next?
Sailor: The wind tugged at our sails, lifted us into the air, and carried us over the town.
Reporter: Did you think you were going to get down safely?
Sailor: No, I was surprised when we landed in the swimming pool.
Reporter: Well, I guess you were lucky to get back in one piece.
Sailor: Yes, we were very lucky.

B. Rewrite each sentence. Add commas if necessary.

Yes I'd like to go sailing with you.

_____

Don't you have extra life jackets hats and coats on your boat?

_____

Yes but let's stay at home read books and bake cookies instead.

_____

SUMMARIZING the LEARNING Use a comma to set off the words _____, _____, and _____ at the beginning of a sentence. Use a comma after each item, except the _____ one, in a series of three or more.

Name_____

Pretend that you are the person in the picture. Complete each sentence with words that will paint an interesting, exciting picture in the reader's mind.

Standing beside the sea, I could hear

_____

_____

_____

_____

_____ .

From where I stood, I saw

_____

_____

_____

_____

_____ .

With each breath, I could smell

_____

_____

_____

_____ .

I felt _____

_____

_____

_____

_____ .

Name _____

Pretend you are the boy in the story "The Wreck of the *Zephyr*." Finish each sentence.

1. When I was sailing the *Zephyr* through the storm, I saw _____

_____ .

I felt _____ .

2. When I saw the boats sailing through the air, I was amazed! They looked

_____

_____ .

As they sailed by, I heard _____ .

3. The sailor gave me oyster stew. It tasted _____

_____ .

It smelled _____ .

4. When the sailor played and sang, it sounded _____

_____ .

5. When the *Zephyr* flew through the air, I felt _____

_____ .

With a partner, make a chart of the senses. Label the columns *See, Hear, Touch,* and *Taste*. Then add words and phrases you find in your reading. Share your chart with your classmates. When you write stories or poems, use the chart to help you make your writing more interesting.

Name_____

Read carefully the description of the toy sailboat. Then follow the directions.

This sailboat will bring you hours of fun! It is the best sailboat model made today. It has three sails made of real sailcloth. You can name the boat yourself using press-on letters. Then just put the boat in the water. It sails along, and its sails move back and forth. All your friends will want one, too!

1. Find three facts in the paragraph and write them.

_____

_____

_____

2. Find three opinions in the paragraph and write them.

_____

_____

_____

3. Look carefully at the toy boat. Write one more fact about it.

_____

4. Write one opinion you have about the toy sailboat.

_____

Name _____

In the blanks, write whether you would use a dictionary,
an atlas, or a globe to look for the information below.

1. _____ how to pronounce the word *zephyr*

2. _____ a country on the equator

3. _____ the meaning of the word *mizzenmast*

4. _____ what a *quarterdeck* is

5. _____ the shortest route from Los Angeles to San Diego

6. _____ a continent in the Southern hemisphere

7. _____ two rivers that empty into the Pacific Ocean

8. _____ what a *bulwark* is part of

9. _____ which city in Argentina has the most people

10. _____ the names of three oceans

GO ON ➡

Name _____

A. Read the story. Write *dictionary*, *atlas*, or *globe* in each blank.

Anna Maria got a postcard from her cousin Ramón. It was from Bergen, Norway. But where was that?

Anna Maria ran to the _____ to look it up.
"Wish you were here!" Ramón wrote. "You should see the beautiful fiords." Anna Maria didn't know what a *fiord* was.

She needed the _____.
"Send letters to me in Lourdes," Ramón wrote. "I'm heading there tomorrow." What country was Lourdes in?

Anna Maria got out the _____ to look it up.
"You can call me, too," Ramón said. "I'm at the Celsius Hotel. It's pronounced just like the Celsius thermometer." Anna

Maria needed to look that up in the _____, too.
"My next stop is halfway around the world," Ramón said. "Can you guess where I'm going?" Anna Maria looked

at a _____ to help her make a good guess.

B. Write one more use for each source.

1. a dictionary

_____

2. an atlas

_____

3. a globe

_____

SKILLS AND STRATEGIES INDEX